MAY 2017

-one as in
stone

Carey Molter

Consulting Editor Monica Marx, M.A./Reading Specialist

Published by SandCastle™, an imprint of ABDO Publishing Company, 4940 Viking Drive, Edina, Minnesota 55435.

Credits
Edited by: Pam Price
Curriculum Coordinator: Nancy Tuminelly
Cover and Interior Design and Production: Mighty Media
Photo Credits: Corbis Images, Eyewire Images, Hemera, PhotoDisc

Library of Congress Cataloging-in-Publication Data

Molter, Carey, 1973-
      -One as in stone / Carey Molter.
          p. cm. -- (Word families. Set VIII)
      Summary: Introduces, in brief text and illustrations, the use of the letter combination "one" in such words as "stone," "bone," "prone," and "alone."
      ISBN 1-59197-274-4
      1. Readers (Primary) [1. Vocabulary. 2. Reading.] I. Title.

PE1119 .M627 2003
428.1--dc21   2002038210

SandCastle™ books are created by a professional team of educators, reading specialists, and content developers around five essential components that include phonemic awareness, phonics, vocabulary, text comprehension, and fluency. All books are written, reviewed, and leveled for guided reading, early intervention reading, and Accelerated Reader® programs and designed for use in shared, guided, and independent reading and writing activities to support a balanced approach to literacy instruction.

Let Us Know

After reading the book, SandCastle would like you to tell us your stories about reading. What is your favorite page? Was there something hard that you needed help with? Share the ups and downs of learning to read. We want to hear from you! To get posted on the ABDO Publishing Company Web site, send us e-mail at:

sandcastle@abdopub.com

SandCastle Level: Beginning

-one Words

bone

cone

phone

scone

stone

throne

Max has a bone.

Bess has a cone.

Mary talks on the phone.

A scone is bread.

Andy sits on the stone wall.

The queen sits on her throne.

A Scone
for Slone

A guinea pig named Slone
lives near a stone.

She marks off her zone
with cone after cone.

Slone lives alone
in her zone.

Sometimes she wishes
she had a clone.

Slone tries to call
her pal Ramone.

She wants to offer
Ramone a scone.

Oh no, there's no
dial tone!

So Slone
gets a scone alone.

Slone eats the scone.

Now Slone would like
an ice-cream cone.

Slone gets an ice-cream
cone and eats it alone.

Slone is happy.

She sits on her throne.

The -one Word Family

alone	Ramone
bone	scone
clone	shone
cone	Slone
drone	stone
hone	throne
phone	tone
prone	zone

Glossary

Some of the words in this list may have more than one meaning. The meaning listed here reflects the way the word is used in the book.

clone   an exact copy of something

cone   an object or shape that is round on one end and pointed on the other end

scone   a type of bread, usually with raisins or berries baked in it

zone   an area that is set off for a specific use or purpose

About SandCastle™

A professional team of educators, reading specialists, and content developers created the SandCastle™ series to support young readers as they develop reading skills and strategies and increase their general knowledge. The SandCastle™ series has four levels that correspond to early literacy development in young children. The levels are provided to help teachers and parents select the appropriate books for young readers.

Emerging Readers
(no flags)

Beginning Readers
(1 flag)

Transitional Readers
(2 flags)

Fluent Readers
(3 flags)

These levels are meant only as a guide. All levels are subject to change.

ABDO
Publishing Company

To see a complete list of SandCastle™ books and other nonfiction titles from ABDO Publishing Company, visit www.abdopub.com or contact us at:
4940 Viking Drive, Edina, Minnesota 55435 • 1-800-800-1312 • fax: 1-952-831-1632